23 WAYS to be a great ARTIST

A step-by-step guide to creating artwork inspired by famous masterpieces

Jennifer McCully

For Casa McCully... again.
Jennifer

Illustrated by Doreen Mulryan • Publisher: Zeta Jones
Associate Publisher: Maxime Boucknooghe
Managing Editor: Laura Knowles
Designer: Clare Barber • Art Director: Susi Martin
Production: Nikki Ingram

First published in the UK in 2015 by QED Publishing

Published in the United States in 2015 by
QEB Publishing, Inc.
6 Orchard, Lake Forest, CA 92630

Originated in Hong Kong by Cypress Colours (HK) Ltd
Printed and bound in China
by 1010 Printing International Ltd

10 9 8 7 6 5 4 3 2 1   15 16 17 18 19

PHOTO CREDITS
(t=top, b=bottom, l=left, r=right)

p.6tl, © Dennis Hallinan / Alamy, **p.8t,** © 2015 The Andy Warhol
Foundation for the Visual Arts, Inc. / Artists Rights Society (ARS),
New York and DACS, London, Alamy, **p.10tl,** © The Pollock-Krasner
Foundation ARS, NY and DACS, London 2015. World History Archive /
Alamy, **p.14tl,** © Succession H. Matisse/ DACS 2015. Photo: Collection
University of California, Los Angeles. Hammer Museum. Gift of Mr.
and Mrs. Sidney F. Brody., **p.16t,** Grandma Moses: Over the River to
Grandma's. Copyright © 1973 Grandma Moses Properties Co., New
York. Christie's Images Ltd. / SuperStock, **p.18,** Paul Klee / Getty
Images **p.20,** © Georgia O'Keeffe Museum / DACS, 2015, Georgia
O'Keeffe, Oriental Poppies, 1927, oil on canvas, 30 x 40 1/8 in., The
Collection of the Frederick R. Weisman Art Museum at the University
of Minnesota, Minneapolis. Museum purchase. 1937.1. , **p.22,** Andy
Goldsworthy, **p.24,** © The Estate of Alberto Giacometti (Fondation
Giacometti, Paris and ADAGP, Paris), licensed in the UK by ACS and
DACS, London 2015. Image copyright The Metropolitan Museum of Art/
Art Resource/Scala, Florence , **p.27tl,** Thomas Barrat, Shutterstock.com,
p.30, © Topfoto/Alinari, **p.33tr,** © Christie's Images / Bridgeman
Images, **p.36,** Concentric Circles, 1913 (oil on canvas), Kandinsky,
Wassily (1866-1944) / Private Collection / Bridgeman Images, **p.38**
Alamy, **p.41tl,** © 2015. Banco de México Diego Rivera Frida Kahlo
Museums Trust, Mexico, D.F. / DACS. The Artchives / Alamy, **p.44tl,**
SuperStock / SuperStock, **p.46tl,** Yayoi Kusama, EVERYTHING ABOUT
MY LOVE, 2013, Acrylic on canvas, 76 3/8 x 76 3/8 inches, 194 x 194 cm
Image © Yayoi Kusama. Courtesy of David Zwirner, New York; Ota Fine
Arts, Tokyo / Singapore; Victoria Miro, London; KUSAMA Enterprise,
p.48tr, © 2015 Calder Foundation, New York / DACS London. Image
courtesy of the Hirshhorn Museum and Sculpture
Garden, **p.51tl,** © Tomas Abad / Alamy,
p.52tl, © ADAGP, Paris and DACS,
London 2015, Artepics / Alamy,
p.54tl, © Elaine Lesser / Alamy,
p.56tl, Faith Ringgold © 1990

NOTE TO PARENTS

The projects in this book are of varying levels of difficulty, and some require the
use of tools or materials that should only be used under adult supervision.

**Children should be supervised at all times when using potentially
dangerous equipment.**

The author and publisher accept no liability for any injuries sustained
in making these projects, which are undertaken entirely at your own risk.

Contents

Let's Make a Masterpiece!

Every artist has a starting point: excitement about the way colors blend on canvas; the way clay feels in their hands. Those starting points lead to masterpieces. Following simple steps might seem like an easy task, but it's not the key to becoming a great artist.

As well as mastering the steps, you should try to be as creative as possible and make every artwork your own. You must learn, experiment, and put your thoughts, feelings, and personality into what you create.

This book focuses on some great artists who have made their mark by doing exactly that. They found their own style and made masterpieces to share with the world.

The projects in this book cover a range of different styles and art forms, and show you how to create artwork using a variety of art supplies. Although you are given the steps to follow for each project, the end result will be your own, individual masterpiece! Your own inspiration and passion will shine through.

✳ It is not about having all the right art supplies, it is about what you can do with the art supplies you do have!

TRY NEW THINGS

Don't be afraid to create the projects more than once. Trying new techniques and colors each time in order to master your creativity will bring your art to a whole new level. Be fearless and brave in the art you create.

STEP-BY-STEP

Every project in this book has step-by-step instructions for you to follow. Read through the instructions before you begin, and then re-read each step carefully before you start it.

It's as easy as 1, 2, 3...

The secret to a successful project is proper preparation! That means getting all your materials and tools ready before you begin. At the beginning of every project, you'll see one of these boxes, telling you all the equipment and supplies you need.

you will need

- canvas panel or board
- paintbrushes (various sizes)
- découpage glue
- acrylic paint
- tissue paper
- scissors

TOP TIP

There are helpful tips throughout the book—don't forget to read them!

REMEMBER: SAFETY FIRST!

- ALWAYS ask permission before starting a project
- ALWAYS have a grown-up close by to help
- NEVER use knives, glue guns, or spray cans without adult supervision
- ALWAYS follow safety instructions

Where you see these signs, it means that the step requires tools or art supplies that could be dangerous, so an adult should be there to give you a hand.

Ask an Adult

Think about it

Look out for this type of box throughout the book. It will give you a helpful prod to think harder about the thoughts, feelings, and meanings behind an artwork or style, and give you other ideas to get more out of the projects.

Get your paint ready—it's time to begin!

"EXOTIC LANDSCAPE" BY HENRI ROUSSEAU, 1910

Jungle Adventure

ARTIST FACT FILE

NAME: Henri Rousseau
(Pronounced: ahn-ree roo-soh)
LIVED: 1844–1910
NATIONALITY: French

you will need

- canvas panel or board (project size is 12 in. x 16 in., but you may choose your size). You could use wood, cardboard, or heavy paper instead.
- acrylic paint (various colors)
- paintbrushes (various sizes)
- matte découpage glue or glue stick
- 3D clear glue dots
- plain, handmade, or scrapbook paper
- pencil and eraser
- scissors

Henri Rousseau is most famous for his colorful oil paintings of jungle scenes. He taught himself to paint and, because he used a "naïve" or childish style, many people thought his work was no good. However, over time his work became more popular, and today Rousseau is seen as a great artist. His busy paintings often look as though they are made out of lots of flat layers, so why not try making a jungle collage in Rousseau's lively style?

1. With acrylic paint, brush on a nice blue background for the sky and some green grass. It is always best to let one background color dry before adding another color on top of it.

2. Once your background is completely dry, draw a tree and paint it using a small brush.

TOP TIP

If you're painting on cardboard or wood, paint the background white first, so the colors are more vibrant!

3. While your tree is drying, paint a quick coat of some bright colors on heavy paper. These will be used for leaves, flowers, and any animal you choose.

4. Once both your tree and hand-painted paper are dry, you can cut out leaves and flowers from the paper and start creating your jungle.

Don't forget the monkey···

5. Lay your jungle out on the background, then begin gluing pieces in place. Start with your animal so that it can be partly hidden in the background. Use a glue stick to glue the animals, Sun, and flower stems in place.

I made this!

6. Finally, use 3D glue dots on the bottom of each plant or flower to stick them down. The glue dots will give your plants a raised look, making your jungle seem more real. As you stick on more layers, watch your jungle come to life!

Pop Art Bag

MARILYN PRINTS BY ANDY WARHOL, 1967

ARTIST FACT FILE

NAME: Andy Warhol
LIVED: 1928–1987
NATIONALITY: American

you will need

- canvas tote bag
- sturdy cardboard (to put inside the bag while painting)
- masking tape
- ruler
- pencil and eraser
- fabric paint (various colors)
- medium-sized paintbrush

TOP TIP

You may need to wash your tote bag before working on it. Follow the instructions that come with your fabric paint.

A ndy Warhol became famous for painting and screen printing images of everyday items such as soup cans and Coca-Cola bottles, as well as celebrities such as Marilyn Monroe (above). He would print the same image over and over, using different bright colors. In this project, you can use your own hand to make a printed bag inspired by Warhol's art.

1. Insert a sturdy piece of cardboard inside the tote bag. This will stop the paint from bleeding through to the other side of the bag.

✴ Make sure your masking-tape square is large enough to fit four of your hand prints inside.

2. Using masking tape, make a large square on your tote bag. This will give your artwork a neat edge.

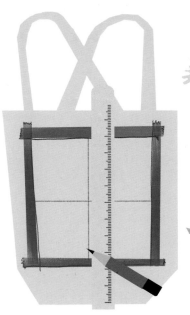

3. Using a sharpened pencil and a ruler, lightly divide the larger square into four quarters—one square for each color.

Think about it

Andy Warhol didn't just use realistic colors in his prints—a person's hair could be yellow, blue, or green! How many colors could you use together on a bag? You could make a whole set and give them to friends and family.

Wash your hands between each color!

4. Paint in each square with a different color fabric paint, using a medium-sized paintbrush. Let the paint dry completely.

5. Using contrasting colors, make hand prints on each square. Let these dry completely. Once the fabric paint has dried, gently remove the masking tape.

"REFLECTION OF THE BIG DIPPER" BY JACKSON POLLOCK, 1947

Splatter Placemat

ARTIST FACT FILE

NAME: Jackson Pollock
LIVED: 1912–1956
NATIONALITY: American

Jackson Pollock is most famous for his huge, expressive paintings, created by dripping trails of paint across a canvas laid out on the floor. He began to number his artworks instead of naming them, so that people wouldn't try to look for particular images in his painting—they would just experience the painting itself.

you will need

- canvas fabric (approximate placemat size: 14 in. x 18 in.)
- scissors
- white gesso or white acrylic paint
- paper cups
- acrylic paint (various colors)
- Paintbrushes (various sizes)
- palette knife
- tar gel (optional)
- pouring medium (optional)
- iron (optional) (adult supervision required)

1. Cut your canvas fabric to size. The size used in this project is based on a standard-sized placemat.

TOP TIP

Always ask an adult first if it is okay to work where you are planning. This is a messy project, so make sure you wear old clothes and spread out plenty of newspaper or a plastic sheet to protect your work surface.

2. To prepare your background, use a large paintbrush to coat the fabric entirely with a layer of white gesso. Let it dry completely.

Think about it

Before you start your splatter painting, try to think of a strong emotion—it could be happy, sad, excited, frightened, loved, angry—whatever you like. As you choose your colors and decide where you want to dribble your paints, try to feel this emotion, and see if you can make it show through in your finished artwork.

3. Now the fun begins! You can start with whatever color paint you wish. Water down your chosen color in a paper cup and then drip some of this paint onto the placemat with a medium-sized paintbrush.

4. After you've made a few marks, add some pouring medium to the paint in the paper cup and mix them together really well. Now pour the paint onto the placemat in a loop-like pattern. Let your first color of paint dry completely before moving on to the next step.

✿ Try not to move your project during the drying times so that your paint does not shift or drip off the edge of the placemat.

5. When the first color of paint is completely dry, you can add a second color. It can give a strong impression if you choose a color that is very different from the first one, such as black and yellow. Add whatever color paint you've chosen to a new paper cup and then add a roughly equal amount of tar gel. Mix them together well.

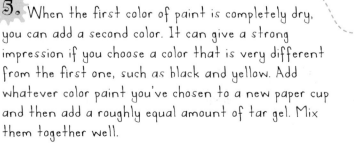

Time to get really messy...

drip paint

6. Use the tip of a palette knife to drip the paint mixture all over the placemat. Let the paint dry before moving on to the next step.

✳ Tar gel makes paint stringy and allows you to get fine lines while dripping with the end of a paintbrush or palette knife.

drip more paint

7. After your second color is dry, go ahead and add your third color! In a paper cup, add some water to the paint and begin dripping the watered-down paint over the placemat with a medium-sized brush. Let your third paint color dry before moving on to the next step.

✳ Try to drip right on top of the areas where you want the paint to fall, without dribbling any paint trails from the cup to the right spots.

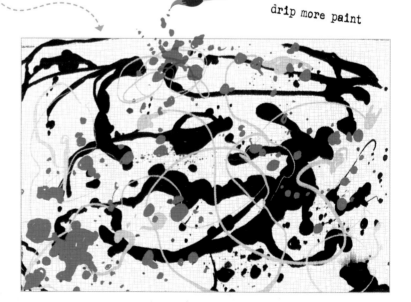

8. Now it's time for the last paint color, and it's also the messiest part of the project! In a paper cup, water down your last paint color even more than you have done with the other colors. Using a medium paintbrush, flick the watered-down paint across the placemat. Start at one end of the placemat and then switch to the other end. Once you are satisfied with your color pattern, let it dry completely.

flick brush

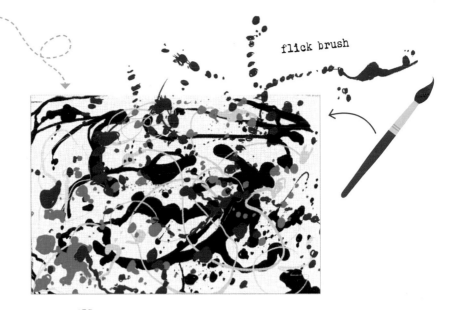

9. Once your paint is completely dry, you may need to lightly run an iron over the placemat to get it to lie flat. Flip your placemat over to the side that has no paint on it and, on a low heat, run the iron over it a couple of times until it is completely flat.

Ask an Adult

Time to turn it over and admire your work!

Think about it

Show your placemat to someone else. Can they guess what emotion you were thinking about when you made it? If you want to make a set of Pollock placemats, how about trying to make each one show a different emotion?

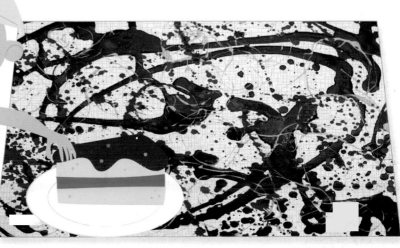

Colorful Cutouts

"THE SHEAF" BY HENRI MATISSE, 1953

ARTIST FACT FILE

NAME: Henri Matisse
(Pronounced: *ahn-ree ma-teece*)
LIVED: 1869–1954
NATIONALITY: French

Henri Matisse was a very successful painter who decided to try out a new way of creating art. Instead of painting, he began to cut out pieces of painted paper and arrange them into beautiful collages. You can make a bold, colorful work of art using this simple technique, just like Matisse.

you will need

- wood, canvas, or sturdy cardboard, around 12 in. x 24 in.
- ruler
- pencil and eraser
- acrylic paint (various colors)
- medium-sized paintbrush
- decorative paper, sugar paper, or specialty handmade paper
- scissors (preferably very sharp scissors with a fine point)
- matte découpage glue

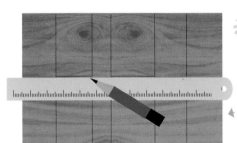

1. If you can find a piece of wood to use, this makes a great base for your project. If not, cardboard will still do the trick!

2. Using a ruler and a sharpened pencil, divide your background up into various-sized rectangles.

3. Choose which colors you want to paint the rectangles, and what color papers you want to use for your cutouts. Think about how the different colors will contrast with each other. You might want to use a variety of bright colors, or you could use just two or three.

4. Once you have chosen your colors, paint the rectangles. Let the paint dry completely.

5. Cut out your Matisse-style paper shapes freely, using a variety of different papers. Create natural shapes that flow and have round edges.

TOP TIP

Use scissors with a very sharp point. This will allow you to create neater, more detailed cutouts.

6. Once you have cut out all of your paper shapes, arrange them on your rectangles and decide where you are going to glue them in place.

7. When all of the shapes are in the position you want, start to glue them down, one by one, using matte découpage glue. It is best to apply this glue using a medium-sized brush. This white glue dries clear and should be used underneath the paper shapes and on top of them, too. It is easy to wash off any glue that gets on your hands, so get sticking!

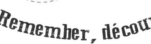

Remember, découpage glue dries clear!

15

Memory Painting

ARTIST FACT FILE

NAME: Anna Mary
Robertson Moses,
known as Grandma Moses
LIVED: 1860–1961
NATIONALITY: American

"OVER THE RIVER TO GRANDMA'S HOUSE" BY GRANDMA MOSES, 1944

you will need

- canvas or wood
- pencil and eraser
- acrylic paint
  (various colors)
- paintbrushes
  (various sizes)

The story of Grandma Moses shows us that it's never too late to become an artist. She left school at twelve to go to work, and later married, had children, and ran her family farm. She only began painting in her seventies, but her art proved extremely popular and was displayed across the United States and Europe. Moses painted scenes of country life—often from her memory—showing farming activities, family, and church. Her nostalgic artwork captures the excitement and joy of everyday life.

Think about it

The scene in this project captures childhood memories of waiting for the big carnival to arrive every spring. Think about some of your favorite memories of everyday activities or special occasions, and pick one to paint from your memory. It might be an activity you used to do, a place you loved to visit, or a trip that you took with your family. Try to capture the things that make the memory special to you.

1. Once you've come up with the memory you wish to capture, start mapping it out on your canvas. Begin by filling in the large background areas.

2. In the scene shown here, the background is a blue sky with clouds, and a green field beneath. Let your background paint dry completely before moving on.

3. Using a pencil, draw your scene's main objects or buildings on top of the background. In this picture, that includes the big fairground rides.

4. Once you're happy with your pencil drawing, start to fill it in with color.

TOP TIP

Even top artists often need to look at photos of real things in order to know how they should draw them. It's very tricky to paint something completely from memory! If you need a helping hand, you can view some images on the Internet to get ideas to help you build upon. Just remember to ask an adult for permission first. Take time to carefully think about what things you want to include in your memory painting.

5. It's now time for your painting to come alive! Begin adding more detail to the scene, such as any people, animals, and other smaller details. In this painting, this included children, flowers in the field, and the balloons floating up into the air. Draw them in with a pencil first, and then add the finishing touches of color.

✻ Just like Grandma Moses did, you don't have to make the people in your scene look perfect. Your goal is to capture the happiness, excitement, or other emotion from your special memory.

17

Cubist Portrait

ARTIST FACT FILE

NAME: Paul Klee
(Pronounced: *paowl clay*)
LIVED: 1879–1940
NATIONALITY: Swiss German

"SENECIO" BY PAUL KLEE, 1922

you will need

- canvas panel or board, wood, or sturdy cardboard, around 12 in. x 16 in.
- white gesso
- acrylic paint (various colors)
- tissue paper, sugar paper, or specialty handmade paper
- scissors
- pencil and eraser
- matte découpage glue or paper cement glue
- oil pastels
- paintbrushes (various sizes)
- black watercolor pencil

Paul Klee was very interested in using color in his paintings, but he had to spend a lot of time practicing and experimenting before he was finally confident in using color. As you can see from his painting, Klee didn't try to paint things exactly how they looked. Instead, he made paintings out of lots of shades of color and different shapes. Have a go at using his style to paint a portrait of yourself or someone you know.

1. Start by giving your canvas a vibrant background. Use two or three different shades of the same color so that it is not one solid color. This will give your background a textured look. Let the background dry completely.

Think about it
Paul Klee made his portrait (above) out of lots of simple shapes. Look in the mirror—what shapes can you see?

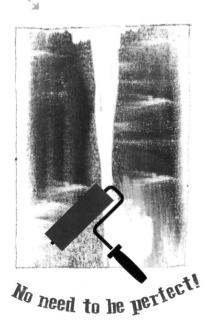

No need to be perfect!

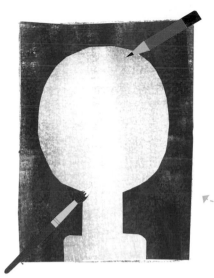

2. Using a sharpened pencil, sketch out the head and neck. Try to use big, strong lines, not fiddly details. Once you are happy with the shape, paint in it with white gesso or white paint. Let the white dry completely before moving on.

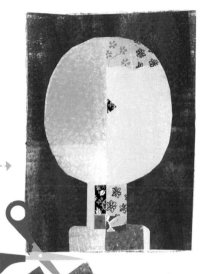

TOP TIP

When gluing paper down, make sure you brush a coat of glue directly onto your background first. Press your piece of paper down firmly, and then add more glue on top. You do not want any corners of your paper peeling up.

3. Now that the face shape is ready, start gluing tissue paper in some areas to add color. Do not be afraid to overlap papers and create layers: this will only make your art more interesting! Fill in the spaces one section at a time, until you are happy with the result.

✻ Remember, découpage glue and paper cement glue both dry clear. You don't need to worry about the glue showing.

4. Once all of the glue is dry, add some small details to finish the portrait. You can add a funky eyebrow or a twisted nose line—a curved line here and there. Don't forget to paint the eyes! Use oil pastels to add more color, smearing the pastel to blend it into other colors. Use a sharpened black watercolor pencil to outline the eyes.

Let the glue dry completely.

Ta-daa!

19

Up-Close Flowers

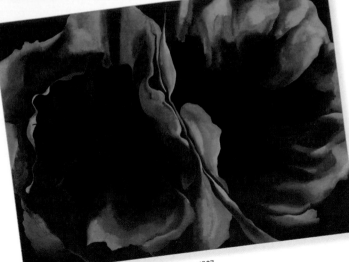

"RED POPPIES" BY GEORGIA O'KEEFFE, 1927

ARTIST FACT FILE

NAME: Georgia O'Keeffe
(Pronounced: *Jor-ja oh-keef*)
LIVED: 1887–1986
NATIONALITY: American

you will need

- thick, rough watercolor paper (about 12 in. x 16 in.)
- watercolor paint (various colors)
- acrylic paint
- paintbrush (medium)
- scissors (preferably with a sharp point for greater detail)
- 3D glue dots
- PVA or découpage glue
- small block of wood

✻ The wood used in this project is 6 in. x 6 in. If you don't have wood, you could use a piece of thick, stiff card stock.

Georgia O'Keeffe was best known for her vibrant oil paintings of flowers, which she painted as though they were being viewed through a magnifying lens. Up close, the flowers looked strange and unfamiliar.

1. To create your own flower, paint blocks of different colors on a sheet of watercolor paper. The color that you plan to use most should take up most of the space on your paper. Let the paint dry.

TOP TIP

When painting your flower, use colors from the same color family. For example, you could paint all reds, oranges, and pinks, or you could paint blues and purples.

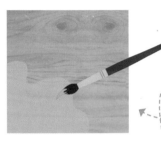

2. Flip your watercolor sheet over and paint the other side the same colors, keeping roughly the same color on both sides.

3. While your watercolor sheet is drying, paint the top and sides of your block of wood with acrylic paint. Let the paint dry.

✻ If you choose a soft, pale color for your wood block, the vibrant colors of the flower will really "pop" off the background.

glue dots

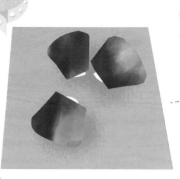

4. Cut out petals in various sizes from your painted watercolor paper. Cut out the larger petals first, and then cut some smaller ones.

5. Start arranging your petals in a flower shape on your wood block, without sticking them down. Cut out some different shapes and sizes of petal, if you need them.

Think about it

Now that you've created a paper flower, why not try painting one, just like Georgia O'Keeffe? You could also paint a really up-close picture of something else, such as a coin, the inside of a piece of fruit, or anything you feel like! Does paying really close attention to an object make you see it differently?

6. When you've cut out your petals, start to glue them down using 3D glue dots. Begin with the larger petals first. To stick each petal down, place a glue dot at one end, on the back side, and press it firmly onto the wood.

7. Once the base of the petal is glued down, bend the paper petal to stick up from the wood block, just like the petal of a real flower. Add more petals until your flower shape is complete.

8. To create the inside of the flower, cut smaller shapes out of your watercolor sheet, using a bold color, such as black. Arrange these pieces and then use 3D glue dots to stick them down.

9. For a final touch, add one last bit of color to the very center of your flower. Cut the piece out of your watercolor sheet, and stick it on using a small dab of glue.

Nature Art

- - - - - - - - - - - - - - - - - - - -
NAME: Andy Goldsworthy
BORN: 1956
NATIONALITY: British

"WOVEN BRANCH CIRCULAR ARCH" BY ANDY GOLDSWORTHY, 1986

you will need
- - - - - - - - - - - - - -
Any natural objects from the outdoor environment, such as:

- colored leaves
- interesting looking leaves
- petals
- pinecones
- stones
- pebbles
- twigs
- seashells
- driftwood
- sand

Andy Goldsworthy collaborates with nature to create his art. He works with what he can find in the natural world: twigs, leaves, snow, ice, reeds, and thorns. As soon as he has finished his creation, he photographs it. He then leaves the artwork in the outdoor environment, to be scattered by the wind, melted, or slowly worn away. The beauty of this type of art, known as "Land Art," is that anyone can give it a go, anywhere. You don't need any extra art materials.

1. Find a good outdoor space to collect materials and create your land art. A great place to start could be your own backyard or a local community park. If you want to use someone else's backyard, ask permission first.

TOP TIP
- - - - - - - - - - - - - -
Don't pick leaves and flowers off their bushes. Instead, pick up the ones that have fallen onto the ground—you'll be giving a new purpose to these with the art that you create, and you won't harm the living plants.

✳ Focus on nature and look at everything around you. This is your chance to arrange nature— however you wish!

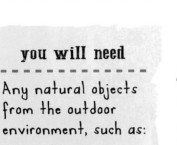

2. Look for some interesting natural objects to use in your artwork. Carefully collect them. You could look for just one type of thing, such as a collection of twigs or leaves, or collect two or three types of things to use together.

3. Think about simple shapes that you can create using the pieces you find—a sun, a moon, stars, swirls, or squiggly lines.

Play with pieces you have. Arrange them delicately, as if "painting" with objects on the ground outside.

Look for natural items that have vibrant colors.

4. As you arrange them, the shape of your art will take form and begin to flourish. Continue adding to your land art until you are content with your creation.

Think about it
What other places do you know that would be good settings for land art? If you enjoyed making this project, why not try to make a piece of land art whenever you take a trip somewhere outdoors? You could make one at the beach, in the woods, by a stream, or even on a mountainside. Take a photo of each one.

5. Once your artwork is finished, take a photo. That way, you'll have a record of it—even when the real thing has disappeared.

23

Wiry People

ARTIST FACT FILE

NAME: Alberto Giacometti
(*Pronounced: al-bear-toe jack-oh-meh-tee*)
LIVED: 1901–1966
NATIONALITY: Swiss

The artist Alberto Giacometti focused on creating sculptures of the human figure. But, instead of trying to make his pieces look like real-life people, he made them very long and thin. He once said that he wasn't sculpting a figure, "but the shadow that is cast." Use this project to create your own sculpture inspired by Giacometti.

you will need

- pipe cleaners
- tinfoil
- air-dry clay
- small piece of wood or MDF board
- staple gun (adult supervision required)
- matte découpage glue
- acrylic paint (variety of colors)
- medium-sized paintbrush
- shallow cup of water for finger dipping
- matte or gloss spray varnish (optional)

1. Begin by taking eight pipe cleaners and twisting two together to make each arm or leg.

twist

arm

arm

leg

leg

2. Twist another two pipe cleaners together and fold it in half to make the main body. Leave a loop at the top for the head.

3. Twist the arms and the legs around the body, so the basic figure is complete.

4. It's now time to begin wrapping tinfoil around each piece. Wad up a ball of tinfoil to place inside the loop for the head.

5. Squeeze the tin foil around the pipe cleaners tightly in order to keep it in place.

6. Once all of the pieces are wrapped together and the entire body is formed, staple the tinfoil sculpture in place on top of the wood. The heavy-duty staples will help him stay in place while you cover him with a very thin layer of clay.

Ask an Adult

✻ **Create the feet to be a little longer than usual so that you can staple them onto the base.**

7. Start adding a layer of air-dry clay to the base around the feet first. This part should be covered in thicker clay than the rest of the sculpture, to support the sculpture.

8. Work your way up from the feet to the legs, torso, arms, and head, adding a thin layer of clay on top of the foil. Add water to the clay with your fingers as you work, as this will help keep the clay moist and smooth, and allow it to stick to the foil. Let the clay air-dry completely before moving on to the next step.

✻ **Follow the drying time on the packet of clay.**

25

9. When the clay is completely dry, do not be alarmed if you see some small cracks. Add a generous layer of découpage glue to the entire sculpture, especially where the feet join to the base. The glue should be applied with a medium-sized paintbrush. Let the glue dry completely before moving on to the next step.

GLUE

✻ Adding découpage glue will help to strengthen your sculpture.

Think about it
Some people think Giacometti's sculptures look like people who are far away in the distance. What do you think? Why do you think Giacometti chose to make sculptures of people in this way?

10. It's now time to paint your sculpture. To make it look like it's made from a dark, bluish metal, you can use black paint and three different shades of blue. Using a dry, medium-sized paintbrush, paint on one or two blues at a time, then go over it gently with some black. Repeat this process over the entire sculpture until you are happy with the finished look.

11. Once your painted sculpture is completely dry, you can add a coat of varnish if you wish. This will add an extra layer of protection for your finished sculpture.

Now give your sculpture a title!

Artsy Art Caddy

"MONUMENT WITH STANDING BEAST" BY JEAN DUBUFFET, 1984

ARTIST FACT FILE

NAME: Jean Dubuffet
(Pronounced: zhahn du-bu-fey)
LIVED: 1901–1985
NATIONALITY: French

Jean Dubuffet made many paintings and large sculptures in his own, unique style. He created strange, twisting shapes, surrounded by thick black outlines. His sculptures contain lots of holes and spaces, and some are big enough to walk through! In this project, you can make a Dubuffet-inspired sculpture that doubles as a handy place to store your art materials.

you will need

- sturdy cardboard (white preferred); a piece approximately 3 ft. x 4 ft. will be needed for this project
- craft knife or box cutter (adult supervision required)
- duct tape (white preferred)
- bag of instant paper mache or modeling compound such as Sculptamold
- molding paste
- piece of sandpaper
- acrylic paint (black)
- small paintbrush

Ask an Adult

1. Start by asking an adult to cut up cardboard pieces for you. These will be used to make up the different sections in your art caddy. Make sure you leave two larger pieces of cardboard, one measuring about 9 x 12 in. and one 16 x 12 in. These will form the base of your caddy.

white tape

2. With your pieces of cardboard and duct tape, make a few boxes of different sizes. If you can, use white duct tape, as this will blend in with the final color.

TOP TIP

Before you make a box, think about what you want to put in it. Coloring pens? Paper clips? Make it the right size and shape to fit.

TOP TIP
You can make any shape you want out of your cardboard. Get creative in putting shapes together—you will be amazed at what cardboard and a roll of duct tape can create.

3. Now start to connect your compartments. Play around with the layout before you stick them together, until you are happy with the shape of your caddy.

4. When stacking the sections, add duct tape to join the open edges of the compartments together, as well as the sides.

✼ Add more modeling compound to areas of your caddy where you want to build up a more curved shape.

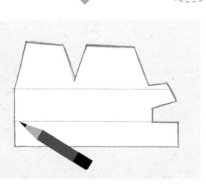

5. When you've added all your compartments, add a back to the caddy. To get the correct shape, draw around the back end onto a larger piece of cardboard and then cut. Ask an adult to help cut the cardboard.

Ask an Adult

Don't forget to wear an apron!

6. Once your caddy is all taped together, you can start adding the modeling compound directly onto the cardboard using your fingers. Follow the directions on the modeling compound package to mix it with the right amount of water. When you have finished adding the modeling compound to the top and sides, let it dry.

7. When your modeling compound is completely dry, it is time to fine-tune the front of your caddy. Using a small paintbrush, add white molding paste to the very front areas of the caddy, where you can see the edges of the cardboard.

8. Cover up any areas that still look like cardboard. The molding paste is perfect for filling in these small areas. Let the molding paste dry completely before moving on to the next step.

9. After the molding paste is completely dry, take a small piece of sandpaper and gently smooth out any very rough areas, to make the curves of your caddy more round and smooth. Brush off or use a vacuum cleaner to suck up any dust after sanding.

10. To complete your art caddy, add some thick, black lines. Let your lines go on an adventure, traveling from one end of the caddy to the other, and connect them to other lines along the way. Follow the curves of the caddy's surface. Let the paint dry completely.

11. Fill your art caddy with whatever supplies you have!

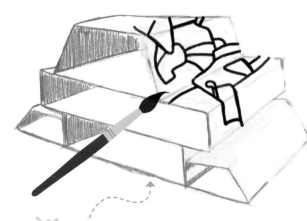

Funny face

BRONZE SCULPTURE BY FRANZ XAVER MESSERSCHMIDT, AFTER 1770

ARTIST FACT FILE

NAME: Franz Xaver Messerschmidt
(Pronounced: franz zay-ver mess-er-shmidt)
LIVED: 1736–1783
NATIONALITY: German

you will need

- air-dry clay (about 1 lb, depending on sculpture size)
- clay tools (basic set)
- smoothie straws
- stapler
- scissors
- duct tape
- tin foil
- shallow cup of water for finger dipping
- greaseproof paper
- acrylic paint (copper)
- paintbrush
- PVA/découpage glue
- square of corruguated cardboard for base (optional)

The sculptor Franz Xaver Messerschmidt is famous for creating many bronze and stone 'character heads' that showed a variety of dramatic, exaggerated expressions. Traditional sculptures of heads often show quite neutral, relaxed expressions, so Messerschmidt's style really stands out from the crowd. Pull your own funny face and have a go at sculpting it in clay.

1. Begin making your head scupture by creating a strong, stable base. Cut a small bundle of large straws to around 2-3 in. long, depending on how big you want your sculpture to be. Wrap them tightly with a strip of duct tape to hold them together.

2. Place two uncut straws in an 'X' shape, and staple them together in the centre. Duct tape them to the staw base. This will be the head shape on top of the neck.

* Building a base means you won't have to use a large amount of clay to make your sculpture. If you prefer, you can skip steps 1 to 3 and sculpt your head out of a solid ball of clay instead.

3. Wad up a ball of tin foil and place it inside the two arched straws. It should be a snug fit.

Think about it
Messerschmidt practiced his exaggerated expressions in the mirror, and used them as inspiration for his sculptures. Pull some funny faces in the mirror, and pick one that you want to try and sculpt. Will your sculpture look surprised, angry, or laughing? Maybe it will be grumpy or silly. Look carefully at the shape your forehead, eyes, nose, mouth, cheeks, and chin make.

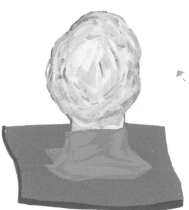

4. Now put tin foil all over the basic head and neck shape. If you choose to use a cardboard square as your base, it is best to duct tape the neck to the cardboard so that the whole structure is stable and doesn't move while you are sculpting.

✣ Create your sculpture on a sheet of greaseproof paper so that the clay doesn't stick to your work surface.

5. Your base is finished, so now you're all ready to sculpt. Dip your fingers in some water and grab some clay! Smooth it onto the tin foil base, starting at the bottom and working your way up.

6. Once you've covered the whole head with clay, start molding the eyes, nose, and mouth. Mould the shapes with your fingers, and make sure they are firmly and smoothly attached to the head.

TOP TIP
It is so much easier to work with wet clay than it is to try and sculpt something that is too dry! Make sure you keep dipping your fingers in water as you sculpt to keep the clay soft and moist.

7. To make the hair, use your hands to roll pieces of clay into thin sausage shapes. Add them to the head one at a time, using a small amount of water and your fingers to smooth each one on at the base

TOP TIP

You can find YouTube videos online that show you some sculpting techniques. Search for "sculpting clay faces." It's a great way to see what's possible if you love using clay and keep on practising!

8. Once you are happy with the basic expression and features, you can use a clay tool to carve out details such as eyes and nostrils. Perhaps you could carve eyelashes, too.

9. When you've finished your sculpture, leave it to dry.

GLUE

❋ If you don't have clay tools, you can use cutlery and a pencil to smooth and indent your sculpture.

10. Some cracking can occur with air-dry clay, so adding a coat of decoupage glue or PVA glue can be helpful to fill any cracks. Using a medium-sized paintbrush, add a coat of glue over the entire sculpture. Let the glue dry completely.

11. If you made your sculpture on a cardboard base, you can trim the edges of the cardboard to give it a nice, neat shape.

12. To add the finishing touch to your sculpture, give it a coat of copper-colored paint. The copper paint will provide a nice, metallic finish and really bring your sculpture to life.

Now give your sculpture a title!

Cubist Notebook

"GUITAR ON A TABLE" BY JUAN GRIS, 1916

you will need

- corrugated cardboard
- craft knife or box cutter (adult supervision required)
- decorative stencil (optional)
- pencil and eraser
- ruler
- acrylic paint (various colors)
- paintbrushes
- watercolor pencil or oil pastel (black)
- matte spray varnish (optional) (adult supervision required)
- grommet pliers or heavy-duty hole punch (adult supervision required)
- three metal binder rings

Ask an Adult

Juan Gris was one of the first artists to paint in a style known as Cubism, a way of painting people and objects as though from many different viewpoints at the same time, breaking down the object into different shapes. This was a very new and exciting way of painting, and inspired many other artists. This project shows you how to make a notebook with a cubist cover so you can jot down all your arty ideas.

1. With adult supervision, cut your cardboard pieces to size.

✳ The sketchbook size for this project is based on the size of large blank index cards (5 x 8 in.).

2. Add a coat of white paint to one side of each card. These will be the front and back covers.

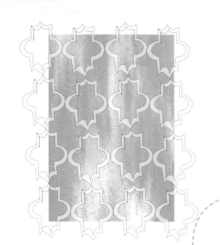

4. When your stencil design is completely dry, add a second color. Let that color dry, too.

* Using two colors will help give extra depth to your artwork.

3. Once the white paint has dried, you can get started on the background. Add some color before you sketch out your main image. You could use a stencil to make an interesting pattern. Don't forget to paint your back cover, too!

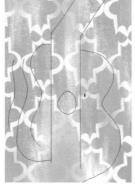

5. Using a ruler and a sharp pencil, draw a three-dimensional, yet simple, shape of your chosen object. Remember to think about the different parts of your object and the different viewpoints you can show.

6. Once your drawing is in place, start to fill in certain areas using paint. There is no need to color the sections of your image the same color—you could paint each section a slightly different shade. Play with painting certain areas darker or lighter. Let the paint dry completely.

Think about it

Gris painted a number of guitars in a Cubist style, but for your notebook, you could choose to draw any object you like on the cover. Why not draw your favorite musical instrument, or another object to do with your favorite hobby? To show your object in a Cubist style, think about how it could be "broken up" into different parts, and drawn from different viewpoints. It doesn't have to look exactly like the object does in real life—you can give it a fresh, unique look!

7. Once your whole image is colored in and the paint is dry, it's time to outline some of the areas to make them stand out. Using a black, sharpened watercolor pencil or an oil pastel, outline a few of the main lines and shapes, and add in some details to your image.

✻ Don't forget to do a back cover, too.

back cover

front cover

✻ Rub your finger over any black lines that you want to blend into the rest of the artwork. Leave other lines clean and straight.

8. If you've used any watercolor or oil pastel, you'll need to varnish your artwork to protect it from being smudged when touched. Ask an adult to help you spray varnish over the covers. Do this outdoors, so that you don't breathe in any of the spray. Let the varnish dry completely before moving on to the next step.

9. Once your artwork is completely dry, it is time to make the three holes for the metal rings. Use a pencil to mark where you want the three rings to go on your covers. Using grommet pliers or a heavy-duty hole punch, punch holes in your front and back covers. Do the same for your blank index cards. Make sure that all of your holes line up.

Ask an Adult

10. Place your index cards between the front and back covers, and put the metal rings through the holes to hold everything together.

Your Cubist-style notebook is now ready to use!

GLUE

"SQUARES WITH CONCENTRIC CIRCLES" BY WASSILY KANDINSKY, 1913

Colorful Coasters

ARTIST FACT FILE

NAME: Wassily Kandinsky
(Pronounced: va-silly can-din-ski)
LIVED: 1866–1944
NATIONALITY: Russian

you will need

- four 4 x 4 in. stone or porcelain tiles
- acrylic paint (various colors)
- paintbrushes (various sizes)
- varnish (adult supervision required)
- small round felt or cork surface protectors

Wassily Kandinsky was an abstract artist with a brilliant eye for color. To create eye-popping artwork like him, you need to know your way around the color wheel—a wheel of colors that shows the relationship between primary, secondary, and tertiary colors. Two colors from opposite sides of the wheel are called complimentary colors. In Kandinsky's famous painting *Squares with Concentric Circles*, some of his circles are bold and jump from one color to the next, while others stay within the same color family.

1. Thoroughly rinse the tile coasters under running water to rinse off any dust. Lay them on a towel to dry. Make sure both sides of the tiles are dry before painting them.

Think about it

Create a color wheel just for fun before starting this project, and see what colors you like best together. Try out as many combinations of colors as you can!

color wheel

✳ The tile coasters used in this project are 4 in. x 4 in. and are Tuscan porcelain. They can be found in DIY stores and typically come in sets of 8 or 12. Tumbled stone tiles can be used as well.

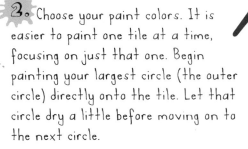

2. Choose your paint colors. It is easier to paint one tile at a time, focusing on just that one. Begin painting your largest circle (the outer circle) directly onto the tile. Let that circle dry a little before moving on to the next circle.

✱ **Acrylic paint will go directly onto the tiles, so there is no need to prepare the tiles with sealant.**

3. Continue painting the rest of your circles until you have reached the center.

4. Now, paint the remaining edges of the tile—this is the color that will act as the square's background.

TOP TIP

Using a varnish will protect your artwork when the coasters are put to use. The varnish will act as a sealant so that the paint is protected. You can use a matte or gloss spray varnish, but you must ask an adult to help you. Make sure you spray the varnish outdoors, so that you don't breathe in the fumes.

5. Continue this process using different color combinations on each of your tiles.

Ask an Adult

6. When your tiles are completely dry, varnish each tile.

7. Once the varnish is dry, add small felt or cork surface protectors to the bottom of each tile. This will stop any furniture you put your coasters on from getting scratched.

Stencil Street Art

"GIRL WITH A RED BALLOON" BY BANKSY

ARTIST FACT FILE

NAME: Banksy
BORN: 1973
NATIONALITY: British

you will need

- paper (plain white and card stock)
- pencil and eraser
- black marker pen
- access to a scanner or photocopy machine (if possible)
- sharp scissors or craft knife (adult supervision required)
- protective board or mat for cutting
- wood, canvas panel, or art paper
- acrylic paint (various colors)
- paintbrushes (various sizes)
- small paint brayer (roller)

Banksy is a graffiti artist who has a distinctive and very popular style of spray painting images onto sides of buildings, walls, and other public places. He mostly works in black and white, with only a hint of color. Because graffitiing other people's property without asking is illegal, Banksy has kept his identity a secret.

❋ Focus on the basic shape and the areas that will be shaded, not on the small details.

1. Look in books, magazines, or on the Internet to find an image that you would like to make into a stencil.

2. Draw or trace the image onto white paper, simplifying the shape so that it will be easy to tell what areas will be cut out for the stencil.

3. Once you are happy with your drawing, make a photocopy of it.

5. Once you have traced your drawing in black, make another photocopy of it.

4. Trace over the photocopied drawing with a black marker pen. Fill in all of the areas that you want to be painted when you use the stencil to make your final artwork. The black, shaded areas are the bits that will be cut out.

6. It is now time to make the stencil itself. Using the photocopy of the black marker-pen image, carefully cut out all the black areas with either scissors or a craft knife. Try to cut your areas out as neatly as possible so that when using the stencil, you get a good, smooth copy of your drawing.

✳ Ask an adult before you use a craft knife or sharp scissors.

Ask an Adult

TOP TIP

Take your stencil one step further! To make your stencil sturdier so you can reuse it, trace your stencil onto a thicker piece of card stock and recut the stencil.

Never use your stencil to graffiti something you aren't supposed to!

✳ Gently stick down the tape.

7. Now that you have created your stencil you can use it on whatever you want. White card stock, canvas, or a wooden board will work well. Place the stencil sheet where you want the image to be on your artwork. Use a small paint brayer to roll paint over the stencil.

❋ If you do not have a small paint brayer, you can use a foam-tip brush or a medium-sized paintbrush over the stencil instead.

8. Once all areas of the stencil are covered with paint, remove the stencil sheet and let your image completely dry.

Think about it

Banksy uses his art to make a statement about social and political issues. You could add a message, such as "PLEASE HELP!" to this panda graffiti, to remind people that pandas are endangered. Can you think of an image you would like to stencil to make a statement about something that is important to you?

PLEASE HELP

9. Once your stenciled image is dry, it is time to add some finishing touches. If you've only used black paint on your stencil, you could add a dash of color. Here, green bamboo has been added.

❋ This project shows how to make a stencil of a panda, but you can use the guidelines on any picture you like. Pictures with a strong contrast between light and dark areas work best.

PLEASE HELP

Personality Portrait

"SELF-PORTRAIT WITH THORN NECKLACE AND HUMMINGBIRD" BY FRIDA KAHLO, 1940

Frida Kahlo taught herself how to paint while recovering from a terrible bus crash. She is best known for her colorful self-portraits that featured images to do with her own life and the troubles she was going through. Her artwork was also influenced by native Mexican art and often focused on her identity as a Mexican. Like Kahlo, paint a portrait that lets your identity shine through.

you will need

- canvas board or canvas stretched on wood
- pencil and eraser
- acrylic paint (various colors)
- paintbrushes (various sizes)
- white gesso
- decorative stencils (optional)
- watercolor pencil (black or brown)
- varnish (adult supervision required)

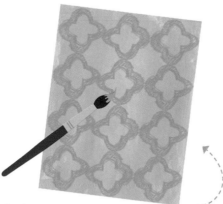

1. Start your self-portrait with a vibrant background color—choose your favourite color, or one that means something special to you. Let it dry completely. Before moving on to the next step, you could stencil a decorative background on top.

Think about it
Frida Kahlo's self-portraits included objects and surroundings that related to her life experiences and were important to her. Think about what objects reflect your personality, interests, and life experiences, and include them in your self-portrait. Have fun, and make it colorful!

41

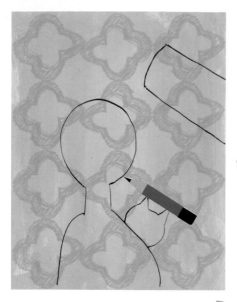

❋ When creating your background, don't just make it a solid color! Use different shades—this will give it more depth and make it individual to you.

2. Using a sharpened pencil, draw the basic shapes that will be the main focus in your portrait: a head, shoulders, and any other objects.

3. Now paint in your shapes with white gesso. Doing this will mean that when you paint the pictures over the top, the colors will be bright and the background color won't show through. Let the gesso dry completely.

4. It's now time to sketch out the facial features and hair. It is important when creating a face that the eyes are lined up correctly. It helps to create basic oval shapes for the eyes, making a third oval shape in the center.

5. Create a fourth oval vertically underneath the middle oval, so that your eyes and nose line up correctly. Last, the mouth should line up directly under the nose. Once you are happy with the way the eyes, nose, and mouth look, erase the extra pencil marks around those areas. Try to erase as much of the unnecessary pencil marks as possible.

6. Begin adding color to the face. Don't forget to add your eye color to the eyes and a little bit of color to the cheeks, if needed.

✱ Instead of using a single shade for your hair, try blending different shades together so it doesn't look flat.

TOP TIP
- - - - - - - - - - - - - -
It is always best to varnish your artwork in order to protect it, especially if you've used watercolor pencils, crayons, or pastels, as these will rub off on your fingers when touched. Make sure you varnish with adult supervision and outdoors, to avoid inhaling the fumes.

7. Start coloring in the other blank spaces. You can use thick, opaque colors such as browns and yellows for hair, so you don't need to paint the background white first.

✱ Watercolor pencil can smear, so be careful!

8. Your self-portrait should be starting to come together. Once the larger areas have dried, begin painting in the details.

9. Using a sharpened watercolor pencil in dark brown, you can outline the eyes and lips, and you can add some small lines for eyebrows and any other little details.

43

"STARRY NIGHT" BY VINCENT VAN GOGH, 1889

Starry Night Painting

ARTIST FACT FILE

NAME: Vincent van Gogh
(Pronounced: vin-sent van gokh)
LIVED: 1853–1890
NATIONALITY: Dutch

you will need

- blank canvas board or canvas stretched on wood
- pencil and eraser
- molding paste
- acrylic paint (various colors)
- small palette knife (plastic or metal)
- small paintbrush for detailing

Van Gogh's *Starry Night* is one of the most popular paintings of all time. In this painting, Van Gogh's use of large brush strokes created the appearance of movement: the sky appears as though it is swirling here and there, giving the painting a colorful energy. Try out his technique for yourself!

Think about it

In this project, we will use a palette knife and paint mixed with molding paste to achieve the effect of Van Gogh's large brush strokes and create a sense of movement. What other scenes can you think of that you could try painting using this style?

1. Using a pencil, sketch out a version of Starry Night directly onto your canvas. The sky is a collection of swirly lines, crescent curves, and circles.

✳ Paint mixed with molding paste will take longer to dry than paint on its own. Luckily, there is no need to wait until the sky is dry before painting the other parts of the picture.

2. Now begin filling your sky with color. Use a palette knife, molding paste, and three to four different shades of blue. Scoop a little molding paste onto your palette knife before scooping up a little paint, too. Keep the shades of blue separate and add a dab of color here and there as you fill in the sky.

3. Now move on to filling in the tall cypress tree and bright yellow stars and moon. Use two to three different yellows, and a touch of white to highlight areas throughout the entire painting.

4. It's time to paint the little village. With a very thin, pointed paintbrush, outline the village buildings and church with black paint.

5. Fill in the colors of the buildings with a small brush or palette knife. Don't use molding paste when filling in the village. Choose the same blues from the night sky, but this time don't blend them together so that the buildings stand out more. Add hints of yellow and red to show light shining out of the window.

6. Now that some of the molding paste has dried in the sky, lightly go over some of the outer areas and around the swirls with a palette knife and light blue paint, to bring the sky to life.

7. Using a small, pointed paintbrush and black paint, go over any pencil lines that are still visible. Your version of *Starry Night* is now complete!

"EVERYTHING ABOUT MY LOVE" BY YAYOI KUSAMA , 2013

Peculiar Patterns

ARTIST FACT FILE

NAME: Yayoi Kusama
(Pronounced: Ya-yoy ku-sama)
BORN: 1929
NATIONALITY: Japanese

you will need

- sturdy paper gift bag—brown or white
- piece of cardboard for placement inside the bag
- pencil and eraser
- acrylic paint (various colors)
- paintbrushes (various sizes)
- oil paint pens (various colors)
- rubber- or foam-tipped tools or cotton swabs (for polka dot making)

Yayoi Kusama is known for her brightly colored paintings and sculptures that overflow with organic shapes and polka dots. During her long career, she has created paintings, sculptures, and live performances, and even covered entire rooms in polka dots! Kusama's use of vibrant, contrasting colors and patterns creates fun, exciting images: perfect inspiration for a decorative gift bag!

1. Place a sturdy piece of cardboard into your bag. This will stop the paint from bleeding through to the other side while you're creating your masterpiece.

2. Using a pencil, draw flowing, curved, "organic" shapes all over the front side of your bag. Focus only on the larger shapes for now.

✻ Use a gift bag made out of thick, sturdy paper. If the paper is thin, using too much paint could make the bag tear easily while wet.

3. Fill in the shapes with a variety of colors using a small paintbrush. Let your first coat of paint dry completely, then add a second coat of paint to any parts you think need to be brighter and bolder.

4. Once all of the shapes are colored in, paint the entire background of the bag in a contrasting color. Let the background dry completely.

Try to stay inside the lines!

TOP TIP

- - - - - - - - - - - - - - -

Use a rubber- or foam-tipped tool or a cotton swab to add polka dots inside your brightly colored shapes. For bold, black polka dots and smaller details such as spikey borders and flower petals, you can use an oil paint pen.

5. Now add the small details, building up a busy pattern. Make sure that each of your large shapes has a pattern added to it in a contrasting color. Continue this process until the front side is filled with detail and let it dry completely.

Repeat for the other side...

6. Open up your bag to draw and paint on the other three sides. To get a firm background to paint on, fill the bag with books. Place your protective sheet of cardboard inside the bag, between the books and the surface you will be painting.

7. Repeat Steps 2 to 5 all over the rest of the bag. When you draw your shapes, make some of them join up with the shapes on the other sides. Pair the same colors and patterns as you did on the front side, so your pattern becomes one continuous work of art!

Flickering Fish Mobile

ARTIST FACT FILE

NAME: Alexander Calder
LIVED: 1898–1976
NATIONALITY: American

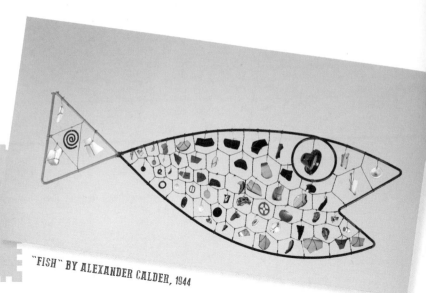

"FISH" BY ALEXANDER CALDER, 1944

you will need

- greaseproof paper
- crayons (approximately 6 crayons)
- vegetable peeler or cheese grater (adult supervision required)
- iron (adult supervision required)
- newspaper
- heavy-gauge wire (16 gauge)
- picture-hanging wire (28 gauge)
- wire jewelry cutters
- wire jewelry pliers
- scissors
- hole punch (smallest size)

Alexander Calder was the artist who invented the mobile: cleverly balanced, kinetic sculptures of wire, sheet metal, and other materials. Some of these works of art were made to move by air currents or electric motor. You can use wire to make all sorts of mobiles, but a great one to start with is a flickering fish to 'swim' in the breeze.

1. Using a peeler or grater, make crayon shavings on a paper plate, one color at a time. Discard any large crayon chunks if you can't grate them any smaller.

2. Lay out a newspaper on your ironing board or work surface.

3. On top of the newspaper, fold a piece of greaseproof paper in half. Place your crayon shavings in between, like a sandwich, so that the greaseproof paper covers all the shavings.

✳ Color will bleed through some of the layers of newspaper. You do not want it to reach your iron or your work surface, so make sure you use plenty of sheets of newspaper.

Ask an Adult

fold over

✳ Six crayons should make around six sheets of wax paper.

4. Place another layer of newspaper on top of the wax paper. With an iron, gently press down one section at a time to melt the crayon wax. Do not pull apart the two sides of greaseproof paper. Let the wax sheets cool completely.

TOP TIP

Do not rub across the wax sheet when melting the crayons like you would a piece of clothing. Press down, section by section, until all of the crayon shavings are melted. This will prevent the colors from smearing too much and making a muddy color.

5. On a large sheet of paper, draw a simple shape of a fish. This will be your template to follow as you create a wire version. Including the tail, the fish shown in this project is about 18 inches long and 10 inches high.

Play with the shape of your fish until you are happy with it.

6. Using one long piece of heavy wire, bend the wire into your fish shape by following your paper template. Where the base of the tail meets the fish's body, the two ends of the wire can be bent into simple hook-like shapes using pliers, and hooked on to complete the shape.

Ask an Adult

7. Cut out scale-like shapes from the cooled wax sheets. These will be your fish's scales.

Ask an Adult

8. Make two or three holes near to the edges of each scale, using a small hole punch.

9. Using thin picture-hanging wire to link the scales, begin to fill in the body of the fish, one scale at a time. Each scale should be connected to the outline of the fish, to another floating scale, or both.

✳ Picture-hanging wire is very thin and easy to bend, but the ends are very sharp and can puncture fingertips easily. Be careful and use pliers instead of your bare hands to shape the wire.

Think about it
Alexander Calder said his wire sculptures were "drawings in space." Once you've made this fish mobile, draw a picture on paper and then have a go at "drawing" your picture in 3D, using a length of wire.

10. Once all of the scales are in place, create a funky hook for the mobile to hang from. Using a length of the heavy wire, curl one end into an interesting, creative hook. Join the other end to your fish, using the same type of hook shape made in Step 6.

Make an interesting hook.

TOP TIP
When connecting scales together with the thin wire, fold the wire in a simple paperclip-type shape. The wax paper scales are very delicate, so you need to take care not to rip them when attaching them to the outline. This part is almost like putting together the pieces of an imaginary puzzle. Create the layout as you go, fitting in a scale here and there.

"GREY WEATHER, GRANDE JATTE" BY GEORGES SEURAT, C. 1886—88

Pointillist Notecards

ARTIST FACT FILE

NAME: Georges Seurat
(Pronounced: zhorzh sur-ra)
LIVED: 1859–1891
NATIONALITY: French

you will need

- blank notecards or watercolor paper cut to notecard size
- pencil and eraser
- acrylic paint or watercolor paint
- rubber- or foam-tip painting tool
- blank envelopes

Georges Seurat's paintings were seriously dotty! He used a style known as Pointillism, in which a picture is created out of many colored dots. Close up, you can just see a lot of dots, but from a distance, the tiny dots seem to blend together. Why not use this style as inspiration for some handmade notecards? You can create any picture out of tiny dots—maybe flowers, an animal, an alien, or a car—your imagination is the limit!

1. With a pencil, very lightly draw your basic shape on the front of your notecard.

2. Using a small rubber- or foam-tipped tool dipped in your chosen color of paint, press down on your paper, one dot at a time, to fill in your shape.

✲ Start by filling in the dots closest to your pencil outline, before filling in the rest.

3. Try to fill in your dots as close together as you can. Use different shades of color. This will add interest to your painting and give it more depth.

4. When the paint is completely dry, gently rub out any pencil lines you can still see.

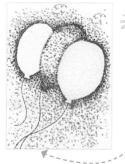

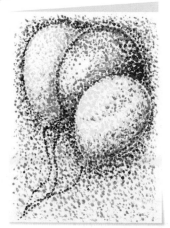

"PERSONAL VALUES" BY RENÉ MAGRITTE, 1952

Surreal Collage

ARTIST FACT FILE

NAME: René Magritte
(Pronounced: ren-ay ma-greet)
LIVED: 1898-1967
NATIONALITY: Belgian

you will need

- canvas, wood, or thick card stock
- images from magazines, catalogs, or newspapers
- sharp scissors (for detailed cutting)
- matte découpage glue or PVA
- medium-sized paintbrush
- black oil pastel (optional)

René Magritte was a Surrealist artist who often painted dreamlike pictures of objects or people in strange places they didn't belong, or in unrealistic sizes. Some of his paintings seemed humorous, while others could be a little unsettling or sinister—sometimes they could be both at the same time! Cutting out different pictures to make a collage is a great way to try making your own Surrealist artwork.

1. Think about what sort of images you might like to feature in your collage... perhaps animals, furniture, plants, or people?

Think about it

Magritte sometimes painted a room filled with small objects blown up to look huge. This made everyday objects seem suddenly strange, and perhaps a little scary, to the viewer. Think about how you could use pictures of everyday things in your collage to make them seem strange and unfamiliar.

* If you don't end up using all of your images, you can use them in your next Surrealist masterpiece!

2. Search for images to cut out of magazines, catalogs, or newspapers. Tear out any pages that you might want so you'll have them on hand when you start to make your collage.

3. Cut out the images and place them on your canvas or card stock.

4. Play with the layout until you have found the scene you want to create. Make sure that the cutouts will cover your background completely, with no empty areas showing through.

✳ Don't start gluing down your collage until you're happy with your composition!

5. When you're ready to start gluing, carefully take all your cutouts off your canvas and put them to one side. Brush a layer of découpage glue over the entire canvas. Gently place your background image on top and press firmly to stick it down.

6. Wait around 20 minutes before adding a layer of découpage glue on top of your background image. On top of this layer, stick down any cutouts that you want to be in the mid-ground of your collage. Press firmly on each image, making sure that they will not peel off.

TOP TIP

- - - - - - - - - - - - - - - -

When your collage is finished and dry, you can rub the side of a black oil pastel over the edges of the painting and blend it in using your finger. This will give your collage a kind of "frame," tying all the cutout images together.

7. After waiting another 15 to 20 minutes, add a third layer of découpage glue. Stick down any cutouts that you want to be in the foreground.

8. Add a final layer of glue on top of your collage. Remember that découpage glue dries clear, so don't worry about being able to see white glue in your final art. Let the glue dry completely.

"COMPOSITION A" BY PIET MONDRIAN, 1920

Abstract Mug

ARTIST FACT FILE

NAME: Piet Mondrian
(Pronounced: peet mon-dree-an)
LIVED: 1872-1944
NATIONALITY: Dutch

Piet Mondrian was an abstract artist with a unique and recognizable style. He painted strong, black lines that joined together to form rectangles, and limited the colors he used to just a bold red, yellow, and blue, along with black, gray, and white. But art doesn't have to hang on a wall—in this project, you'll learn how to recreate Mondrian's striking style on a mug. Drink up!

you will need

- white ceramic mug
- ceramic markers or oil-based paint markers
- washi tape or masking tape
- baby wipes

TOP TIP

The use of washi or masking tape for this project is a great way to keep your lines straight when trying to create Mondrian's style, but it does take time and patience. If you choose not to use tape to create your straight lines, then you can simply draw them freehand.

1. Clean your mug with soap and water and dry it thoroughly before starting.

* If your markers came with baking instructions for your home oven, follow those instructions for baking once your artwork is complete in order to "set" the paint.

2. Put a strip of tape the whole length of the mug, vertically. Using a black ceramic marker pen, draw your first straight line. Wait a couple of minutes before removing the strip of tape. This will ensure that your marker line does not bleed.

3. Add other vertical strips of tape and draw on the black lines, as in Step 2. Make sure you don't place tape on top of any of your black lines, or they will smear. Once you have completed your vertical lines, leave your mug to dry for a few hours, or overnight.

vertical lines

Think about it
Mondrian used the primary colors in his work. Look back at the color wheel on page 36. Which three colors would you use if you were Mondrian. Why?

TOP TIP

It takes one to two days for the oil paint marker to dry completely, so keep the mug upright while painting it to stop it from smearing or sticking to anything. Keep a pack of baby wipes on hand, ready to clean up any marks or smudges from the mug right away, before the paint dries!

4. When your vertical lines are dry, add horizontal strips of tape, and carefully draw on those black lines, as in Step 2. Together, the two sets of lines should form squares and rectangles.

horizontal lines

Leave these lines to dry completely.

5. Now that the black lines are complete, fill in some of the spaces with whatever colors you wish.

6. If you need to color in a certain area again in order to cover up some white areas, wait for the paint to dry for a couple of hours before going back over it again.

"TAR BEACH 2" BY FAITH RINGGOLD, 1990

Story Quilt

ARTIST FACT FILE

NAME: Faith Ringgold
(Pronounced: fayth ring-gold)
BORN: 1930
NATIONALITY: American

you will need

- fabric canvas (about 20 in. x 40 in.)
- pencil and eraser
- cardboard
- ruler or yardstick
- acrylic paint (various colors)
- paintbrushes (various sizes)
- fine-tip fabric markers or oil-based markers (optional)
- thin quilt batting (optional)
- fabric for the back of the quilt if sewing
- sewing machine (optional)
- needle and thread (hand stitching optional)
- masking tape (optional)
- iron-on hemming tape (optional)
- iron (optional)

The artist Faith Ringgold wanted to find a unique way to share her own stories with others. She did this through painting, writing, and sewing on fabric, creating colorful and inspiring works of art. She feels that her quilts are like mini books or stories, with each section of a quilt being like a page from a book. You can make one to tell your own story!

1. Plan what story you want to tell. Choose a size of canvas material that will give you room to paint the main picture, your border, and your words.

Think about it
This project allows you to share your own story with others. What story do you want to tell? Make it bold, so that others will be inspired by your story or message each time they look at your painted quilt!

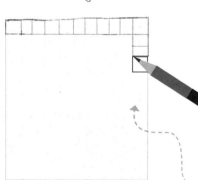

2. Cut out a 2 x 2 in. square of cardboard to use as a template for your border. Place it in the corner of your fabric canvas and draw around the edge.

3. Move the square around the outside of the fabric, drawing around it each time until you have a border of squares.

4. Start painting in a bold color to cover the entire background of what will be your main picture. Paint the border squares in different colors. Wait for the paint to dry completely.

5. Using a sharpened pencil, draw out your story. In the project shown here, the main shapes of buildings were drawn directly on top of the background color.

✱ Don't worry about the pencil lines, as these will be covered up when you paint your story in.

Use a small paintbrush for the smaller details!

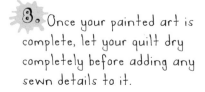

6. When you are happy with your drawing, paint in the buildings. Add the details, such as the windows, trees, and taxi, once the paint is dry.

✱ Fill up your quilt! Try not to leave many blank spaces.

7. Use fabric marker pens or oil-based markers to add details to each colored square in the border. Use a variety of shapes, lines, and squiggly patterns to give each square personality!

8. Once your painted art is complete, let your quilt dry completely before adding any sewn details to it.

10. Place your canvas face-down, and position the thin batting material and fabric for the back of your quilt on top, so that the batting is sandwiched in the middle.

9. To add the quilted effect to your artwork, you'll need to use a sewing machine to sew diagonal lines across your canvas, joining the front artwork to the middle and back layers of the quilt.

Ask an Adult

11. Pin these in place with pins or safety pins.

12. Turn your quilt over so that the picture is facing you again. It's now time to add your first guideline to help you sew straight lines on top of your quilt. Place a long ruler or metal tape measure, diagonally from corner to corner across the middle of your quilt. Stick a strip of masking tape to your quilt along the entire length of the ruler. The edge of your masking tape will be your first sewing guideline.

13. Using a sewing machine, sew along the edge of the masking tape. Once you've sewn a complete line, remove the masking tape and move on to the next line.

Ask an Adult

14. The diagonal lines should be 4 inches apart from each other. Start in the middle of your quilt, with the longest line first, and then add lines on each side. When you've sewn lines across your whole quilt in one direction, do the same thing in the other direction, so you end up with a diamond pattern of stitching.

✱ Don't sew over the masking tape, only along the edge. It's quicker and neater to use a sewing machine, but you can stitch your quilt by hand.

15. To finish sewing the back on your quilt, sew a line all the way around the four sides, about 1/2 inch from the edge.

16. To add words on your artwork, cut small patches of the same canvas material you used for the front of your quilt. Write your words using an ultra-fine-tip fabric marker. This will ensure that your writing stays neat and clean for easy reading.

• There was so much to see!

Ta-daa! Your story quilt is complete!

17. Attach the patches of writing to your quilt by either hand stitching or using iron-on hemming tape. Place the tape all over the back of your fabric patches of writing.

Ask an Adult

18. Position the patches on your quilt. With help from an adult, use an iron to bond the fabric patches to your quilt.

It was our first time visiting the city.

I was excited.

There was so much to see!

The Never-Ending Project

MY ART JOURNAL

ARTIST FACT FILE

NAME: You!
LIVED: Now!

you will need

- enthusiasm
- determination
- inspiration
- fun!

This book has included 22 amazing artists, working in many different styles and using all sorts of materials. Now, it is time to focus on the most important artist of all—YOU!

Hopefully you've had a great time working on these projects, but learning about how to be a great artist doesn't stop when you finish a book: it's a never-ending project! To keep track of all your great artwork and to help you build on your skills, keep an art journal. Here are some top tips for what to put in your journal.

1. Write down your ideas, emotions, and things that inspire you. You can look back at them later and use them as a starting point for a piece of art.

2. Take photos of your artwork, and keep them in your art journal. Looking back at your photos will help you see the progress you've made as you become a more confident artist.

Artist's treasure box

Keep a box of found objects, pretty paper scraps, and anything else that might come in handy. You never know what you might want to include in your artwork.

3. Photos also help you remember the decisions you made when creating your artwork. Would you do something differently next time?

4. Cut out and collect pictures from magazines, newspapers, and catalogs. These can give you lots of ideas to get you started when you need a creative boost.

5. Collect and take photos of objects you find when you're out and about, such as interesting leaves or feathers.

6. It's nice to have a journal you can hold and carry around with you, but you could create an art journal on a computer, tablet, or online, instead. Different journals work for different people!

TOP TIPS

- **Find your style**—what makes your art look like you created it. The more you practice, the stronger your style will be.

- **Try** working with lots of different materials and find out which ones you enjoy most.

- **Be fearless**—try new techniques, explore colors, and use tools and materials in different ways.

- **Tell your story**—personalize your art by including your own thoughts and feelings in it. This will bring your art to life.

- **Jump right in**—make a simple mark to get your artwork started. This will get you over that first bit of fear of starting a project. Once your art is complete, you might not even see the initial mark you made, and that is okay.

- **Make mistakes**—it's part of being an artist. Giving things a go will help you learn and improve. Sometimes, a mistake makes an artwork even better!

- **Never stop creating**—practice makes perfect.

THE ULTIMATE TIP

The most important tip for becoming a great artist is to have fun. Maybe you'll become a famous artist one day. Maybe you won't! In the end, being a great artist is about creating art that makes you happy.

Glossary

abstract type of art that doesn't try to show things as they really look, but instead focuses on colors, lines, and shapes

acrylic paint artist's paint that can be used thickly or mixed with water to thin it down. Different colors of acrylic paint can be blended together to make other colors and shades.

blend mix together

canvas strong cloth that is used as a surface to paint on. Normally it has been coated in a white base coat, ready for painting, and is either stretched on a wooden frame or stuck onto a thick cardboard panel to make a canvas board.

collage artwork made by arranging and sticking down pieces of paper, photos, magazine and newspaper cuttings, and other materials to create a new image

color wheel a circle split into sections showing different colors so that the user can see which colors are similar to each other (next to each other on the color wheel) and which colors are most different (opposite each other on the wheel).

complimentary color a color that normally works well when used next to another color in an artwork. Complimentary colors sit opposite each other on the color wheel.

contrast being very different from something else. Dark and light are contrasting, as are rough and smooth.

Cubism type of abstract art invented in the early 1900s, where the artist tried to show an object or person from many different veiwpoints at the same time

découpage glue type of glue used for gluing layers of paper onto a surface. It can also be used as a varnish and sealant on paper, clay, and painted surfaces. Mod Podge is a widely available and easy-to-use découpage glue.

experiment try something out

expressive showing a thought or feeling

gesso type of thick, white paint used as a base layer to prepare a surface for painting

graffiti images or words painted onto buildings, walls, and other spaces, often using spray paint

image picture or representation of a thing. An image could be a photograph, drawing, or painting.

influence having an effect on someone or something

medium material that an artwork is made from, for example, clay, acrylic paint, pencils or pastels. More than one medium is called 'media'.

molding paste medium used to add texture to a painting. It is also called modeling paste.

naïve art simple style of art made by an artist who has had little or no artistic training

opaque not see-through

pouring medium liquid that is mixed with paint and poured onto a canvas or wood panel rather than painted on using a brush or palette knife. When the paint is dry, it has a glossy effect.

primary color one of the three colors that can be mixed to make all other colors. The primary colors are red, yellow, and blue.

screen printing way of printing in which a special kind of stencil is made on a fine mesh screen. Paint is then pushed through the screen onto a surface to make the artwork.

sculpture three-dimensional art, made out of clay, metal, stone, or other materials

secondary color color that is made by mixing two primary colors together. Green is a secondary color made by mixing yellow and blue. Orange is made by mixing red and yellow. Purple is made by mixing blue and red.

shade darkness or lightness of a color. For example, sky blue is a lighter shade of blue than navy blue.

style particular look that artworks by an individual artist or group of artists has that makes it clear they are by the same person, or linked by similar ideas and ways of working

Surrealism type of art started in the 1920s that dealt with showing dreamlike ideas

tar gel colorless gel that is added to paint to make it stringy. It is used for dripping paint onto a surface in fine lines.

technique way of doing a particular thing

tertiary color color that is made by mixing together either a primary and secondary color, or two secondary colors. Tertiary colors are blue-green, yellow-green, yellow-orange, and so on. They sit between the primary and secondary colors on the color wheel.

texture the way something feels. For example, sandpaper has a rough texture, but glass has a smooth texture.

vibrant bright; vivid; full of energy

Index